Career-Ready Kids

CARE FOR COMMUNITIES

Diane Lindsey Reeves

21st Century Junior Library

Published in the United States of America by:

CHERRY LAKE PRESS
2395 South Huron Parkway, Suite 200, Ann Arbor, Michigan 48104
www.cherrylakepress.com

Reading Adviser: Beth Walker Gambro, MS, Ed., Reading Consultant, Yorkville, IL

Photo Credits: © Prostockstudio/Dreamstime.com, cover; © Streamlight Studios/Shutterstock, 5; © imorarash/Shutterstock, 6; © Kzenon/Shutterstock, 7; © Media_Photos/Shutterstock, 8–9; © Pixel-Shot/Shutterstock, 10–11; © Dmytro Zinkevych/Shutterstock, 13; KATRIN BOLOVTSOVA/Pexels.com, 14; © LightField Studios/Shutterstock, 16; © Gorodenkoff/Shutterstock, 19

Copyright © 2026 by Cherry Lake Publishing Group
All rights reserved. No part of this book may be reproduced or utilized in any form or by any means without written permission from the publisher.

Cherry Lake Press is an imprint of Cherry Lake Publishing Group.

Library of Congress Cataloging-in-Publication Data has been filed and is available at catalog.loc.gov.

Cherry Lake Publishing Group would like to acknowledge the work of the Partnership for 21st Century Learning, a Network of Battelle for Kids. Please visit Battelle for Kids online for more information.

Printed in the United States of America

Note from publisher: Websites change regularly, and their future contents are outside of our control. Supervise children when conducting any recommended online searches for extended learning opportunities.

CONTENTS

Chapter 1: Discover the Caring for Communities Career Cluster — 4

Chapter 2: Explore Caring for Communities Careers — 10

Chapter 3: Is Caring for Communities in Your Future? — 17

Activity — 21
Glossary — 22
Find Out More — 23
Index — 24
About the Author — 24

DISCOVER THE CARING FOR COMMUNITIES CAREER CLUSTER

How can I help? The Caring for **Communities** career cluster from the National Career Clusters® Framework answers this question in many ways. People who choose these careers see a problem for people. Then they help solve it. Some of these workers teach kids how to read and learn. Others keep communities safe. Still others work to keep people healthy and well.

Careers that care for communities have been around you your whole life! Can you guess what a few of them are?

All of these careers help people. Some focus on education. Some focus on health care. Others deal with people's basic needs. These needs include housing, food, and jobs. Some of these careers focus on public service and safety.

These choices let you match a career to your interests and skills. You get to use your talents. You can use them to make your community better.

There are many different health care careers. Which ones have you seen in your community?

Look!

Look around your community to see caring careers in action. What kinds of careers can you find? Where do helpers work? What problems do these helpers solve?

You also can choose how much training you want to do. Some careers, like doctor or principal, take many years of college. Others, like firefighter or emergency medical technician (EMT), have shorter special training times. Some can be learned with on-the-job experience. Education goals are a big part of choosing a career.

People in social work careers help all over the community. They are in homes, schools, and hospitals.

8

Let's explore the three Caring for Communities career areas:

- Education
- Health care and human services
- Public service and safety

Create!

Use words and drawings to create a picture of your dream caring career. What problem would you want to solve? How would you help people? What solutions could you offer?

EXPLORE CARING FOR COMMUNITIES CAREERS

Communities everywhere need lots of help. People with helping careers come to the rescue. They do this in different ways.

Education is one way people care for communities. Learning lasts for a lifetime. It starts with childcare for babies. It ends with elder care for older people. And there is a lot of education in between.

Childcare workers get to care for kids at the very beginning of their lives.

Teachers, principals, and other helpers work in schools. Some educators write textbooks. Others create technology for learning. Some work as librarians or clerks in libraries.

Health care careers keep communities healthy. These careers include nurse and doctor. They include **nurse practitioner** or physician's assistant.

Human service careers focus on meeting people's basic needs. These include food, housing, and jobs.

Make a Guess!

What kind of doctor should you see for a check-up for school? What if you have a problem with your teeth? Who would you see if you needed your **appendix** removed? Ask an adult to help you go online to find out about medical specialties.

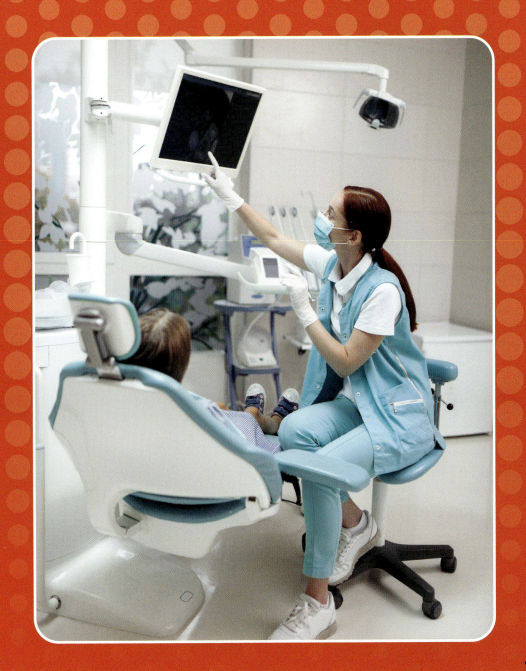

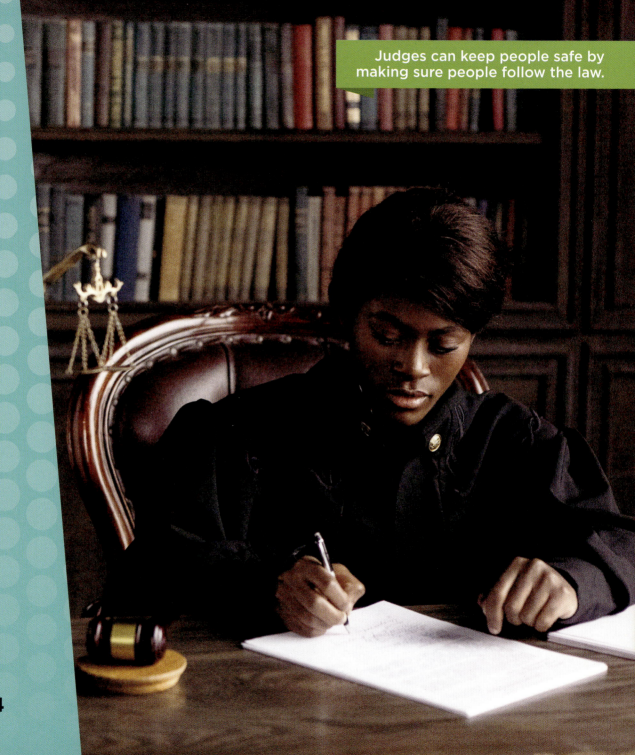

Judges can keep people safe by making sure people follow the law.

Human service workers help out when people are in a **crisis**. Social work and therapy are examples of human service careers. There are many public service and safety careers. These include legal careers like **lawyer** and judge. They also include first responder careers like police officer and firefighter. The military also offers many ways to help keep the public safe.

Are you a problem solver? Do you want to help your community? Consider opportunities in the Caring for Communities career cluster.

Does emergency medical care sound interesting to you? Maybe you want to be an EMT! These are emergency medical technicians.

IS CARING FOR COMMUNITIES IN YOUR FUTURE?

Are you a good helper? Do you like working to solve problems? If your answer is yes, that's your first clue! Caring for Communities careers might be a good choice for you.

There is no rush to decide. But it can be fun to check out the options. Figure out what you like to do. Think of what you want to know more about.

These clues will help narrow down your choices. Learning about yourself and exploring different careers are good ways to be a career-ready kid.

You can experiment with career ideas, too. Ask an adult to help you talk to someone with a career that interests you. An adult can help you visit places where these people work. Think about what the work is like. Imagine the kinds of problems you can solve.

Being a career-ready kid **motivates** you to do your best work now. You can build a bridge from learning in school to preparing for your future career.

Think!

Think about the type of problem you might want to solve in your life's work. What careers would let you be part of the solution? Is it education? Maybe it's health care or human services. Or could it be public service or safety?

Adults around you are in all kinds of careers! Talk to them to see what career may be a good fit for you.

INVESTIGATE CARING FOR COMMUNITIES CAREERS

Safety
- crime scene investigator
- emergency dispatcher
- firefighter
- military officer

Medicine
- chiropractor
- dentist
- doctor
- pharmacist

CARE FOR COMMUNITIES

Law
- lawyer
- paralegal

Fitness
- athletic trainer
- coach
- fitness instructor

Education
- media specialist
- principal
- school counselor
- social worker
- teacher

ACTIVITY

Talk to someone who cares for the community! With an adult, call your local fire station.

- Ask if there would be a good time to come visit to interview a firefighter. Bring questions for the firefighter.

- Find out what is important for community safety. Ask the firefighter how they plan ahead to keep people safe.

- Ask them to show you their equipment and trucks. How do these things help keep the community safe?

Ask Questions!

You can help care for your community now. Maybe you can help pick up litter at a park. Or read books to kids at the library. Ask yourself: How can I help? An adult can help you figure it out. It is good practice for a future caring career!

GLOSSARY

appendix (uh-PEN-diks) a small organ attached to the intestine

communities (kuh-MYOO-nuh-teez) towns or cities and the people who live in them

crisis (KRIYE-suhs) big problem or dangerous situation

lawyer (LOY-uhr) a person who works to help people with legal matters

motivates (MOH-tuh-vayts) provides a person with a reason for taking action

nurse practitioner (NUHRS prak-TIH-shuh-nuhr) a nurse with advanced training and education

FIND OUT MORE

Books
Learmonth, Amanda. *I Like Helping People . . . What Jobs Are There?* Tulsa, OK: Kane Miller, 2021.

Reeves, Diane Lindsey. *Choose a Career Adventure in the Military.* Ann Arbor, MI: Cherry Lake Publishing, 2016.

Reeves, Diane Lindsey. *What Firefighters Need to Know.* Ann Arbor, MI: Cherry Lake Publishing, 2024.

Stocker, Shannon. *Finding the Helpers.* Ann Arbor, MI: Cherry Lake Publishing, 2021.

Websites
Explore these online resources with an adult.

Know It All—Kids Work!: Hospital Series

Mayo Clinic: Careers A to Z

INDEX

activities, 21

career choices, 6–7, 9, 15, 17–20
career clusters, 4–5, 9, 15
childcare careers, 10–11

education careers, 4–7, 9–12, 20

health care careers, 4–7, 9, 12–13, 16, 19–20
helping careers, 4–21
human service careers, 8, 12, 15, 20

interests, 6–7, 9, 15, 17–21

learning and training, 7, 18
legal careers, 14–15, 20

medical careers, 4, 6–7, 9, 12–13, 16, 19–20

problem-solving, 4, 15, 17–18
public service and safety careers, 6–7, 9, 15–16, 20–21

social work careers, 8, 15, 20

training and learning, 7, 18

volunteering, 21

ABOUT THE AUTHOR

Diane Lindsey Reeves writes books to help students of all ages find bright futures. She lives in North Carolina with her husband and a big kooky dog named Honey. She has four of the best grandkids in the world.